BROWNE

PUBLISHED BY
LAPWING PUBLICATIONS
c/o DENNIS & RENE GREIG
1 BALLYSILLAN DRIVE
BELFAST BT14 8HQ

TYPESET BY
LAPWING GRAFIX
c/o BRIAN CHRISTIE
51 KILCOOLE GDNS
TELE: 712483

PRINTED BY
REGENCY PRESS BELFAST

ISBN 1 898472 06 8

LAPWING POETRY PAMPHLET
FRED JOHNSTON: BROWNE
PUBLISHED 1993
COPYRIGHT REMAINS WITH AUTHOR

THIS IS THE FIRST PUBLICATION

OF THE REVISED TEXT OF BROWNE

Lapwing Publications gratefully acknowledge
the financial assistance of the **Arts Council of
Northern Ireland** in the publication of this
pamphlet.

FOR BRID

BROWNE

I'm going mad, he thought,
it's gone too far
following teenage lovers through
Belfast in a car
ignoring traffic-signals, crossings,
cops
even Army checkpoint stops -
and he was thinking this when a shock
of lights struck him
and he stared through his windscreen
up the barrel of a gun.

Window down, Browne,
new rain on his right shoulder,
older by the minute,
driver's licence to a bespectacled
squaddie,
eyes squinted in the glare
Browne watched
the black muzzles dripping in the rain
peeping out from under camouflage
rain-capes, and somewhere
the hoarse whimper of a radio.

Browne drove on, crept
past a personnel-carrier that muttered
to itself, doors open, black
inside as night,
and he'd lost all sight of his lovers,
they'd gone to cover
down a lane, up an entry,
over there by the docks
or back up by the City Hall -
he wanted to crawl away and weep
or stop the car and go asleep
and behind him the squaddies
stopped someone else.

Browne was forty-one, a teacher,
in love with one of his pupils,
a clean, transcendent sort of love,
unspoken, unfulfilled,
the stuff of the poems he drilled
into them, which killed his own
quite personal pain
and all he knew was seeing her again
and again did him no good and made
him happy,
which his wife had not done, which his
life did not do otherwise.

He was not a fool, and knew
that she brought back some remnant
of a previous age
some blank page upon which he might,
at a former stage, have written
and her face had savaged him with
adolescence, her own and his,
every expression, word, frown
conspired, it seemed
to desanctify Browne,
strip him of his above-it-all holiness,
(he thought his secret was all over town)
until, a well-lapsed Catholic,
he went into a church and sat down.

Guilt, then, and sin
and the wages of sin
and the billboards and handbills and
Saturday sermons the Protestants loved,
their missionary zeal
ignoring the way real men feel -
he'd lived in this city all his life
and thought the Protestants well-
dressed and funny,
with some odd notions of God above
and here he'd met his wife.

Browne loved his job and did it well.
She hadn't understood
his delicate vocation
she'd thought him jelly, and said so,
and sex didn't turn him on,
and she wouldn't be surprised
if he used men's magazines, filthy stuff;
it was all years too rough
and he was glad it was over
and he left her the semi and childlessness
and retired at thirty-eight
to a landlady and BBC Northern Ireland
and boiled eggs with melted butter.

Browne bought The Irish News in the
mornings, read the headlines in the staff-
room and passed the paper on;
coming home it was The Belfast Telegraph
for T.V. and sport, for Browne had a child's
interest in football, being all East Belfast,
The Oval terraces on Saturdays with his
father and uncle, flat-capped shipyard men
who could wring a joke out of thin air -
and he'd go away and pee under the stands
and clap his hands like a wind-up monkey
when Glentoran scored.

All dead now. Maybe all that old team,
for all he knew. Browne visited the family
grave and brought flowers, noting with
curiosity
how his parents had the same surname as
himself,
driving back down into the city,
tilting his head to see Napoleon's neb
up on Cave Hill -
gantries to the foreground like stubble
on Boney's chin,
starlings round City Hall, his Da showing him
the Covenant signed in blood,
one tribe digging in forever and ever Amen.

He'd wanted children, so he had:
Browne was a natural Dad, glad to be
around kids, lifting them up and swinging
them until they squealed with delight,
and whether it was his wife's fault or his
he never knew,
but something stale grew up between them
and that was that,
and if he felt her sobbing in the sheets
beside him, he said nothing, didn't move,
could not upset grief's applecart, no -
grief was to be expected.

The landlady, plump and eager, aproned
and in flat slippers, was all the corner-
women he'd known from childhood,
the Newtownards Road, Albertbridge,
arms crossed, they'd discuss the world
and raise shipyard workers and - much later,
a single lifetime - the casual dead
and those others who'd emigrated
for no other reason than lack of work:
Templemore, Ballyhackamore, something wept
in Browne when he drove there these days,
on days off and half-days when he had
unplanned-for time on his hands
and he'd visit the badlands of his childhood.

His landlady brought him tea and Hovis (sliced)
and told him with a shout upstairs
when the News was on
and spoke in whispers at breakfast
and he was her only tenant
and they were insignificantly happy
together, she almost eighty -
she felt proud and respectable having
a teacher to board,
Browne felt hardly anything
and was happy with that.

And into this harmless world without end
his mad love had entered
by some back door Browne hadn't shut
through some riddle of her own
she'd made herself manifest,
conjured up one afternoon
out of thirty-odd, bored, sticky, limp-eyed
schoolkids,
the ineluctible tang of menstruation
and soap,
she had risen up more terrible than the sun.

He'd heard of this phenomenon, had Browne,
and wondered
and felt the questions too unharmonious
to ask,
and there was no one to ask
and he dreaded some imbecile's guffaw
and felt vaguely threatened by the onset
of sin and sin's fires,
so kept it all to himself,
reminding himself at morning prayer
that her hair was not newly-washed for *him*,
of whom, beyond his teacherliness,
she was unaware.

And his desires were vague,
all soft green gardens and a timelessness
around her like a fog
he himself might watch but not participate,
and an Oriental dog prancing
beside her, long days, high walls, a lute
pure Boccaccio -
Christ! but she didn't belong here,
with the windows all steamy and every second
face acned - her own quite flawless -
and outside barbed-wire around the
basketball yard:
not a unicorn or conical hat to be seen.

Daft, it was, Browne told himself,
but he was already dead.
He had walked from one room into another,
heard laughter and sought it's cause,
glimpsed a rose explode on a dunghill
and his life was over. He read them
through Wordsworth and Keats and thought
of Dante,
heard the bell close out their day
and closed his eyes.

He turned up the street this day
and the gates were closed,
the kids were everywhere, schoolbags,
pouts, Punk hairstyles, Army boots,
pleated skirts, clandestine cigarettes -
and the Army were in the playground,
heavy jackets, sleek guns, a weird beauty,
and the street was cordoned off and
a couple of millies from a biscuit-factory
idled their teabreak away in floury aprons.

Bomb scare, said Mawhinney, (Science), all
tweeds and pipe-smoke; love to lock
the bastard in, bomb and all, if I caught him.
But Browne cast around him for
a gentler fish,
and saw her, found her with his hooking eye,
leaning against a motorbike
arm-in-arm with a wee hard in a leather jacket;
and they were going nowhere,
there were no bombs
and the garden was all around them.

The yard was gravel-black
through the rusty railings: Browne
   watched the Army's robot scuttle
to the school's big front doors and saw
the motorbike
and the way she teased him, this
leather-sharp wee brush-head
whose language (most probably)
was common as dirt
whose manners needed mending
who (most likely) had bad teeth and
smoker's breath, her heart in his oily

appentice-dosser's hands.
Browne felt the soldier's firmness
push him back with a 'Right, now, Sir',
and saw the others back-step
like some choreographed stage-movement
and thought he saw,
but maybe he didn't,
the leather-jacket kiss her full on
the mouth,
chancing his arm, as lovers do,
at the moment when the world's nerves
are stretched tightest.

Mawhinney, known to drink,
disappeared. The street was half-cleared,
pupils whispering as if sound
alone would detonate the thing, the
human voice, kids' voices too -
he watched her despite the Army's
caution, watched her as the soldiers
broke them up; and the biker wheeled
alongside her, happy enough, and she was
raising her Belfast schoolgirl's squeal,
less rescuable than before,
the product of pragmatic times.

There was a silence then
that consumed time,
a savage coldness, a split atom -
and then the thud, like schoolbooks
dropping off a desk, of the bomb going off,
a trickle of smoke, nothing more,
filtering through the flung-wide front
door, and a sharp hysteric scream here
and there which died unattended -
Browne heard someone say 'Well , that's over ',
and found his mouth was dry.

Dreams came to Browne,
the tail-ends of dreams
(the Army packed it up, rolled
away tidily war's apparatus),
and a thin rain fell over Black Mountain,
over Divis from the Antrim Glens,
last refuge of Gaelic
in Ulster's North East -
snippets of dreams, as the pupils
straggled home each side of him,
they had the day off at least.

He stood there, immune
to the world and the new rain,
his head was wet again,
baptised into dreaming, childhood
resurrected, a stumbling thing,
but at last it came through:
Browne felt a queer panic tickle
his throat,
chewing Cookstown sausages he sat
in short trousers,
his mother put spittle on her
fingers and smoothed back his eye-lashes.

At the bus-stop Browne waited
while a dozen girls giggled in knee-socks
and blazers - Protestant girls, beautiful
and unreachable - and Browne
had bad acne
and tried not to face them,
but he wanted to, dearly, just once
to be loved by them:
'Don't squeeze your pimples, the girls'll
all see them,' his mother had warned him
as he ploughed strips of marmalade
into Kennedy's bread.

He'd loved one of them once,
asked her out for a walk:
I can't go with you, you're a Catholic,
she'd said,
and Browne had felt something inside him
go dead -
and three decades later her words
hammered in his head (is *her* boyfriend
a Catholic? I trust he is, thought Browne):
and at once he felt a wave of shame
rise up and drown him.

She was gone when he looked,
he was almost alone,
save for the women in door-
ways gossiping and watching him,
like the thief he was, stealer
of children's love;
if there's a God, thought Browne,
He's too far above me
to help me now,
and he walked to his car.

As Browne might have guessed
their love had gone underground,
the gangster in leathers picked her up
out of sight two streets away,
she'd pretended to dander off idly
and there she was, lithe legs over
the black seat, and they were off
into traffic -
Browne shut his wipers down
as the shower eased away (gone South,
down by Queen's Bridge, up Castle-
reagh)
and he was watching and driving.

And driving and watching
until the road-block got in his way
and he lost them -
he drove through his city,
composing a fantasy in verse,
taking his mind off thoughts
that were very much worse and rhymed
with viciousness -
he saw car parks where shops had been
remembered how much he'd loved
Kennedy's American Donuts and Walls
ice-cream,
a dream of love and a child stamping
his feet: I want, I want.

When I was a lad
I went with my Dad
and we always got clad
at Spackman's -
he'd looked up over the door and read
his first poem that wasn't Wordsworth
or Shelley or that bloke that wrote
about Nelson (what was his name?): Graves -
while his father negotiated his first
pair of long trousers
passport to a troubled kingdom
and he remembered how the Albert Clock
always leaned a little
and the prossies posed outside the pubs.

All dead now, Browne mused
as he drove,
all dead or old and the men who picked
them up dead or old
and I am both -
I was scared, so scared, always scared,
he remembered
and the first time a girl kissed me
and sighed I asked her if she was feeling
sick -
something tricked me into the man I am,
there were lies in my dreams back then
and I never grew up; or grew up to soon.

Browne parked his car neatly,
meticulous as always, and put the key
in the door-lock and opened it
to the smell of frying:
'Mister Browne, son, you're wet
and you're home awful early the day' -
and her face and her voice were so like
his own mother's he wanted to weep,
no, rush to her first,
have her arms around his shoulders
to heal him, assure him, that God
loved him yet.

'Will you have a wee bite, son? I'm
having a fry and I know you like
sausages':
waddle, in worn slippers, apron with
flowers, odour of soap and something less
tangible,
a comforting balm,
a nectar, a salve
which came out of her naturally
more potent with years -
Browne wiped away tears which he quickly
called rain,
though the rain was in Downpatrick now
and drenching the Mournes.

He ate and they talked in the half-
dark kitchen, and she watched him,
mouth anticipating his words:
'It was on the wireless,' she said -
the word *radio* meant nothing to her -
'Shocking, I call that, the poor wee
childer.'
'Aye', answered Browne; 'but sure they
were delighted to have the day off.'
'All the same,' her mouth told him (he
felt his chin, lightly, for acne),
'them'll put bombs in a school, son,
how will they answer their God?'

She cleared off the table, he buttered
his Hovis, sipped tea with his shoes off,
a double-bar heater crackling
in the fireplace -
and he felt at ease again and drummed
with his fingers and smoked a Players
and listened to her humming a lullaby -
he slept, and she left him there,
as he knew she would, old mother,
time's guardian, keeper of secrets,
watcher at the gate of his soul.

A door opened and in Browne stepped;
a garden, high walls, and a stillness
and brightness -
and Browne felt at home, light-headed
but healthy -
was it Boccaccio? A letter, Giovanna,
now you are my wife; I will leave it here,
you will read it
you are the life-blood within me,
and how long have I loved you? There
is no age
to the love penned on each page.

Above the wall, gantries, arrogant
and still
awaiting the twist of eternal gears,
motionless, listening:
the letter dissolves
and the gantries shudder and hum -
he opens his mouth
and nothing comes out, he tries
to run but he runs on thin air,
snagged on a branch heavy with berries
his sleeve rips
he sees her there, her face

turned away, looking elsewhere
into some obscure distance,
the geographies change, they are
hemmed in by railings, rusting and angry
spiked and peeling - and he runs
and is snagged again, his arms hanging
naked to a wild garden of roses,
brambles, harsh bushes -
he remembers her name, says it once,
then is silenced
by a squaddie in leathers.

Browne is out of the garden
in a street of wee houses
red-brick and geraniums
No Hope Here
written high up in whitewash -
and she's there again, smiling
a child's eyes staring
right through him
to some place inside him
where a wee lad in short trousers
hides his pimples, hides
and is hidden
by this gawky schoolteacher

who pretends he can't see her:
she laughs in his face, then touches
his arm, flesh to flesh,
she says, 'It's only Mr Browne,'
and he falls off the edge of the world
as he has constructed it,
gantries and gardens fall into one
another,
there are bells in the background,
churchbells sounding Sundays
over chained-up playgrounds
and shuttered public-houses -
and he's in the back seat and his

father driving:
'If the weather holds we'll go as far
as Donaghadee' -
her fingers on his arm, perspective
suspended -
'Come with us! Come with us!', or,
'Let go of my arm, it'll catch
in the door!':
let go, let go,
decide, decide,
I'm sorry - and they drive off without
her, leaving her standing where
he could have been kissing her -
and he couldn't forgive them, hearing
her sighing, he couldn't stop crying.

'Mister Browne, are you sickly?'
His landlady over him; 'I've been tugging
your arm, you were muttering terrible'.
Browne takes in the room, sees
the window, fresh sunlight;
'I'll be grand in a minute, bad dreams,
guilty conscience,' -
he hopes that she'll laugh, and she does,
at his quip -
'Mister Browne, you're too saintly a man
to have nightmares'.

Twenty years and I'll die,
the same age as my father -
he was parking the car again, a misty
bad morning -
the schoolyard was jammed with them,
pushing and shouting,
a normal beginning, a day without promise,
Mawhinney looked flushed, and the others
merely stupid,
herding the kids as if they'd no directions
of their own,
more luck to them.

The same body sweat, the odour of women,
in a corridor lighted by genderless neon:
twenty years, then it's over,
she'll have kids of her own, some
will sit here where she sat,
if all comes to all -
Mawhinney edged up to him:
'There's some of those wee girls've eyes
for the men, Browne, you don't mind me
saying it, they're growing up fast,
there's no way of watching them,
if you get my meaning, once they get
out there'.
'Sure that's not our problem anyway,'
said Browne.

The room where the bomb had been
was boarded and closed, Browne stalked
to his classroom and watched them
file in,
it was always the same, let them settle
in their own good time, then wait till
they're seated, then call out the roll -
he opened the ledger and told himself:
I've got poems to give her,
in secret,
my gift to myself, there's a garden
in each of us, she's no exception,
if I can't go there
then someone else must.

Chalk dust and Shelley,
Browne turns his back and wipes away
yesterday
with a slightly-damp cloth -
he was calling their names out,
more anxious each minute, when the door
opened and in she came,
out of breath, guilty; his own Beatrice -
'I'm awfully sorry, Mister Browne,' she said,
standing -
they watched him, he felt it,

they'd peeked over the wall,
or something, he knew it
by the instinct he'd developed -
and one or two sniggered
and he stared them into silence:
'She's been out all night courting,'
he heard from the distance, and
they sniggered again:
'Sit down, let's get started' -
the professional man, the impersonal
teacher Browne knew he was
took over, and shook him; and

as she walked off to her desk
in the corner, Browne
recited his litany, accusing,
begrudging: I am old, I am dead,
and the world spins around me
oblivious to who I am, what I am,
and why,
I am not of their kingdom,
they've branded me *outcast*
I've no passport on me, I never had
one
that could take me on through.

I am Browne, merely Browne,
a teacher of English
in a town in the news;
but myself, I'm not news,
simply one among thousands
who survive daily dreaming
of girls they'd have loved
if they'd been someone else -
I am chalk, I am duster, I am
rhymes learned by rote
I am the mote in their eye.

Browne paced up and down
as they bent over Shelley, or someone,
that Graves bloke, he couldn't think
straight:
he came alongside her desk,
her closeness
was all that day had for him,
then he paced on and stooped,
took a petal, half-
curled up, withered,
from the floor right beside her,
a rose petal, red, fragile
and mysterious,
sacred, to Browne.